Sanibel Island is a sunny island. It is off of the gulf coast of Florida. Herons, spoonbills, pelicans, osprey and wood storks fly above.

Fish jump in the bayous. Alligators, lizards and raccoons roam.

Sanibel Island

The Everglades →

ISBN 978-1-934582-45-9
Library of Congress Control Number 2011912154
Published by Back Channel Press, Portsmouth, New Hampshire

Printed in the United States

The Strange Tale
of the
Determined
Crocodile

Carol Zall Lincoln

Illustrated by

Randon T. Eddy

Some people said, "Go home, Wilma! Crocodiles don't live this far north. Go back to the Everglades."

Some people called
her Wilma.

She traveled through
Sanibel's waterways and
lived mostly in a special
place that was her home.
It is called the J.N. "Ding"
Darling National Wildlife
Refuge.

Some people called her
Wilma.

She moved to
Sanibel Island
some forty
years ago.
She was nine
feet long and
ten years old.

Some people
called her
Wilma.

The people treated her well.
They watched her.
They watched out for her.

Wilma weathered many storms,
hurricanes and cold weather.

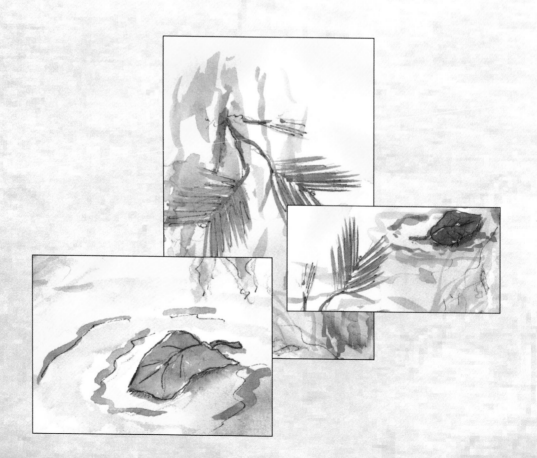

Some people thought she should live in the Everglades. The Florida Everglades was a safer place for crocodiles to live.

Three times the Florida Wildlife Officer took her back to the Everglades. Each time she found her way back to Sanibel.

She was a very determined crocodile.
Some people called her Wilma.

There were plenty of turtles, raccoons, birds and small alligators to eat.

She built nests and laid eggs
every year for twenty years,
but none of her eggs ever hatched.
She laid eggs in unusual places.

People came to watch over them.

They placed barricades across the road at night so cars wouldn't run into her while she was resting in the middle of the road.

Some people called her Wilma.

One time she chased a female alligator away and adopted her sixteen newly hatched baby alligators for five days. Then the mother came back.

People kept records and reports of her comings and goings.

One day a newspaper was delivered to a house that was much too close to her nest. So the very protective croc mom picked up the newspaper in her teeth and delivered it to the front door where it belonged.

The "Ding" Darling tram driver always tipped his hat to her when she was basking in the sun along Wildlife Drive.

Some people called her Wilma.

Bike riders waved to her on their journeys through the Ding Darling Reserve.

People always respected Wilma. After all, she was a wild and dangerous reptile. They stayed a great distance away from her.

January 2010 was an unusually cold month in Florida.

January 26th was a sad day. It was a very cold morning. Wilma was found dead on the pathway to the conservation center.

She was a very old, cold-blooded animal. Cold-blooded animals can't live for very long in cold weather. They are different than warm-blooded dogs, cats and people.

Hundreds of alligators and other reptiles died in southwest Florida during those unusually cold days.

Sanibel residents were sad and shed many tears. They had lost their most famous crocodile resident.

Some people called her Wilma.
Most people loved Wilma.

A memorial service was held one afternoon on the porch of the Sanibel Captiva Conservation Foundation.

Wilma's many friends came and told stories and shared pictures of her.

All of the 200 guests toasted her with Gatorade and said goodbye to Sanibel's most determined crocodile.

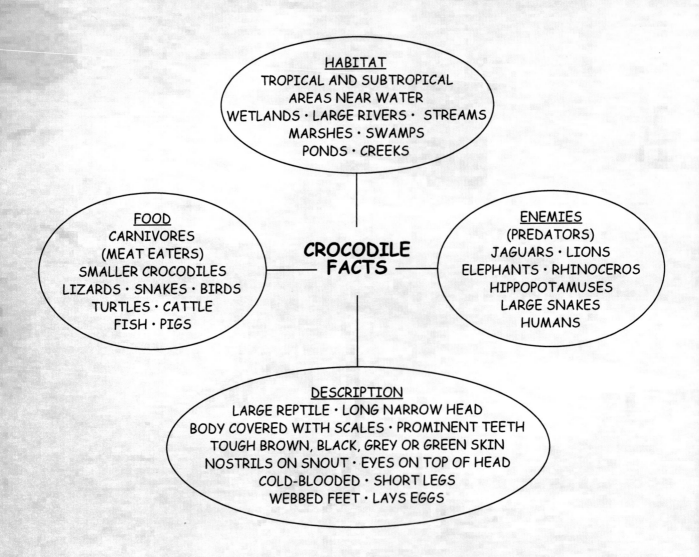

HABITAT
TROPICAL AND SUBTROPICAL
AREAS NEAR WATER
WETLANDS · LARGE RIVERS · STREAMS
MARSHES · SWAMPS
PONDS · CREEKS

FOOD
CARNIVORES
(MEAT EATERS)
SMALLER CROCODILES
LIZARDS · SNAKES · BIRDS
TURTLES · CATTLE
FISH · PIGS

CROCODILE FACTS

ENEMIES
(PREDATORS)
JAGUARS · LIONS
ELEPHANTS · RHINOCEROS
HIPPOPOTAMUSES
LARGE SNAKES
HUMANS

DESCRIPTION
LARGE REPTILE · LONG NARROW HEAD
BODY COVERED WITH SCALES · PROMINENT TEETH
TOUGH BROWN, BLACK, GREY OR GREEN SKIN
NOSTRILS ON SNOUT · EYES ON TOP OF HEAD
COLD-BLOODED · SHORT LEGS
WEBBED FEET · LAYS EGGS

CROCODILE FICTION

Bill and Pete to the Rescue. Tomie DePaola, 2001.
Cranky the Crocodile. Gavin Delacour, 2009.
Crocodile Listens. April Sayer, 2001.
Crocodile Tears. Alex Beard, 2007.
The Enormous Crocodile. Raold Dahl, 2008.
Have You Seen the Crocodile? Colin West, 2009.
Lyle, Lyle, Crocodile. Bernard Waber, 1966.
Mr. Croc's Silly Sock. Frank Rogers, 1999.

ACKNOWLEDGMENTS

Thank you to all my friends and family who read Wilma
and offered many helpful suggestions.